PITT POETRY SERIES

Terrance Hayes
Nancy Krygowski
Jeffrey McDaniel
Editors

Dragstripping

DRAGSTRIPPING

Scarline

SANCTIFIED

Junkie

JAN BEATTY

Published by the University of Pittsburgh Press, Pittsburgh, Pa., 15260

Copyright © 2024, Jan Beatty

All rights reserved

Manufactured in the United States of America

Printed on acid-free paper

10 9 8 7 6 5 4 3 2 1

ISBN 13: 978-0-8229-6727-9

ISBN 10: 0-8229-6727-8

Cover art by Carlos Hernandez

for Ed Ochester

I was born in a steel mill
I was born in the violations of others
I was born blue
I was born blue
half-aborted by my mother's hands
and a coat hanger
But, who cares?
It's one small almost death, in the many
deaths—
The women killed and never found:
the women killed in their own homes
then disposed of; the women killed by
boyfriends, husbands, partners, strangers:
buried in the dirt of this country—

The unknown bodies of women

Contents

✝

Sanctified

for Sister Rosetta Tharpe

Dear Sister Rosetta,
it's 50 years too late, but I love your high-
heeled guitar playing, the way they said you railed
your white Les Paul Custom like a tommy gun:
gospel-wild and showing the men how it's done—
double cutaway fins, your dress breathing red flowers
hugging your full-size body, and
I don't want to be redeemed, but I
have become glorious in the halls of tricked-
out love from the glint of your enormous necklace,
hearing your soul-heavy voice surge/
flowers blur as your chest swells with
song, I'm blown away by my own bullets of trouble.
Sister, I'm saying what you always knew—
that real is real,
that in the nightclub wailing and the strap-on
guitars, there's no happy ending,
just the blues shouters, scorching,
sanctified.

The Body's River

I was born for betrayal—
When my mother left me in the orphanage,

I invented love with strangers.
And if it wasn't there, I made it be there,

until the crash, the revelation.
They say blues is three chords and the truth—

And poetry is long-lined lies and a deep dive
into the body's costly river.

The Emptying

Rosalia Asylum and Maternity Hospital

Mullions cut the windows
into equal pieces, there were cats
prowling the halls of the asylum.

Nights straight-line rain hit the glass,
the wooden rafters shook.
Oracles in white uniforms scavenged,

lifting us to their rooms under
the heavy crucifix. Searching for prophecy
in our small bodies, they held us

to their flat breasts, drove their fingers
inside us dreaming of jesus:
How he would fuck them, hallelujah!

"Whose seed am I?" the oracles
sang, hovering, as they licked and
sucked in the dark,

emptying everything—
mediums between the dirty town
of the small room and the vast space.

6

2

Drag

with a line from Neil Young

They say I have attachment disorder
from years in the orphanage—I say
I'm attached to dirt: to the grit
of stones, pulverized metal from
the slag heap, I learned touch
from air, I fashioned love from
strangers. Your *families*
make no sense to me.
My mother's the 4 barrel of a 409,
my heart's dragstripped
from the shredded tires
of predators. Go ahead,
think of me—
throw the red flag down.
I'm one you'd never figured,
dead engine start on a quarter-mile strip,
my lo-jack is the split/
the pull away—
you back there,
me running the distance.

Dragstripping

I met a stripper on my first visit to the big West,
sitting on a hill in Marin—I was wearing a black red yellow plaid shirt,
she wore something more open, loose,
sleeveless.
       Her knees to her chest,
she was pulling at the brown California
grass, throwing it back down.
I loved looking at her plain brown hair falling over the side of her face.
I was still wearing women's clothes and shoes,
but I made myself a believer that day.
Her thick belt, heavy boots—brown eyes.

The way she looked at me until I had to look away.
She was boy and I hadn't met anyone like her yet,
look at her blue shirt, she opened me, the way
she tore at the grass: hard then threw it.
We walked the hills in Marin, I wanted
to be like her, I wanted to be her.
I couldn't even say what she had,
but I wanted it.
Our time lasted only weeks, but her face
still comes to me.

I made myself a queen those days,
inside I felt the turning diamonds
of a life not lived/someone else's life,
now mine: holding the vision, heavy as mud,
I thought: *Just a push?*

Into my own bleeding heart—
I could feel the brass screws of the rail's underside/
a train running without me/
I could feel the spikes and the crosscuts
and I came alive in the fading light and the skyful of birds.
And I did, I did—and it was
fierce and wild, and back-to-the-wall scary,
it was off/on, whenever she was there, I was a blank slate
with a hard body, it was everything I wanted,
someone to kiss me nice and slow,
then slam me onto the ground's body.

It would be years until I knew her, knew that part of me
as I searched secondhand stores for men's clothing/
men's size 7 shoes, looking for the boy/man in me.
I don't believe in salvation, but
look at her body stripping:

jerking to one side, head bent,
hair covers her face, breasts large and moving,
her thickness:
Wet with boysweat between her legs,
a stripshot across a pitchblack stage,
flash of a woman running her show.
However she wants you/she can have you/half of a whole
body/stripping for you,
the body divided/
                 against itself

in beauty:
I made myself a man watching her:
the stripshot breaks apart
into millions of shotback stars
cutting the night apart
in her crosscut body,
hard and lovely.

Some people say half isn't anything/
but it will drive an ocean back
to the center.
She'll take your money and you'll thank her
in the cage of your body,
drowning in the stripping/
loving the shotback body.

>   *Dear ghost of everything you wanted:*
>
>   *Jerking you into pleasure, jerking you*
>   *into your own story with a stripshot*
>   *of ammo to the vulva, triangle of light,*
>   *triangle of her: the wrapper, 3 sides of lust,*
>   *the fuckfield, the 4th eye.*

I saw the future in her body but I didn't know my questions:
all that came out of my mouth
were birds.

Junkie

the first day i shot dope
was on a sunday.
       I had just come
home from church
        got mad at my motha
cuz she got mad at me. u dig?

—Sonia Sanchez

There's light along the stripline tonight: this is your new family, same as the old—cold, not there, spot the dealer at 50 ft, shady deal behind the van/side lot, know the city solitaire—5am light after all-night drugs/don't look straight in the eye/movement to the corner/same as the old/don't acknowledge/who to look at & when/ get the dope don't be stupid friendly/shut up & listen/know the main player/walk away/not too far/the way someone holds their head/behind the van/same as the old/study the movement/don't look like you give a shit/night after night/don't acknowledge/they know you saw them already/behind the van/shut up & listen/walk away/not too far/gangster lean doesn't mean gangster/same as the old. cold, not there/get the dope/walk away

When Rape Was an Ocean,

she became larger in it

In the box apartment off the side road,
she said yes, one drink.

She doesn't remember his face,

just the flat boulders on the sandbar, man-made
for protection:

ocean water coming in/
water going out

Follow the line of shore with a string:

She was dropping down,
her body falling

Before the sky star splits, before the water
rolls back into her—

cutting wires of light
cutting wires of light

The line of shore can't be replicated, the string
now gone, her body marked

How she reads water
in the moment of trauma/
there is cutting and there is light

These are her new directions

Don't pretend you can't see this

She swims headlong away
she wants to *be* ocean, wants
to find the sky

She wants to be sky

She swims headlong and larger
headlong and larger
larger

The Drawbridge

Spelling & grammar want me to use *bulkheads*
instead of *fuckheads* & although I like bulk,

there's nothing like the smack of a fuckhead.

Like Jack White, who says *technology is a big destroyer*
of emotion and truth,
                      I dream of sledgehammering computers,
jumping on them, then throwing the detritus out the window—

feeling my own gunfire, because who wants a watered-
down heart?

People call me dark, but a world without dark//
is just half a world.

I know you understand.
There's a bridge between us, can you see it?

Didn't you ever want to tear something down?
Smash it to make the parts talk their battered talk:

the stabbing edges & burning colors, the love compressed
in the steel beam & the raging yellow flame?

Dead a thousand years, & I've never tired
of the dying waving me away:

that last hand lifted between you & me:
that raised drawbridge of power,

that sweet breeze of *that's enough*.

The Stripping Tools

I knew nothing of the stripping tools.
Axes, hatchets. wedges.
Only the throwing stone of anger,
the best aim, the raw finish.

The file blade of the moment,
walking down Murray Avenue in Pittsburgh,
a bottle of cheap Chardonnay
in my right hand, my left stuck out with

thumb raised. Hitchhiking to the
hippie concert on Flagstaff Hill,
only a mile away, but I could hear
the jam bands starting up.

Yellow VW stopped and I jumped in.
Raised the bottle to the driver, a guy
in his 30s with red hair, flaming beard,
and he took a swig.

Where you headed? he said.
Just over the hill to the concert, I said.
Aren't you afraid to hitchhike, he asked,
No, I said, *my car broke down*.

Oh, he said.
He ran his eyes over my summer teeshirt,
he looked back at the road and said,
I have a hatchet under my seat.

Oh, I said, looking at the overhanging
trees. *Do you want to see it?* he said,
turning his head with a curled smile.
No, that's okay, I said, trying to keep

my breathing steady, my chest filling
with wild air, my throat becoming stone.
At the hill's bottom, I flung open the door
and jumped onto the road

and the spirit voices looking down
onto the bodies of war spoke.
I rolled away, he sped away,
and my face in the gray concrete

had me looking at land in a different way:
miles of blacktop, years
of blacktop between
what's right and this—

Who was I at war with?

I cried on the street, weeping with new
waters, drowning in the river of killings
I would later hear:
a man with red hair and beard, stories

of beheading women in PA and West Virginia,
unknown woman   unknown woman
heads found in streams and rivers.
These waters weren't my quest

of deep stripping, but/
the stone axe sharpened for thinning.
Primitive.
Chipping away at the internal weeping.

3

I Ran into Water

Last week I ran into Water on the street,
said, *What's up?*

I'm fighting the dragon, he said, *trying to blend
male and female.
It's a big job*, he said.

Later, at the hairdresser, I said, *Kill it, cut it all off,*
stepping to the measure of my own cavalry.
Because inside my body, there is no home/and I
want to say to anyone:

*It's like there's no body
I can live in,
so I walk around in the one I have.
I'm wearing striker boots
to kick the straight men away,
spit-shined, with heel irons.*

Blues Shouter

I'm covering myself with clothes—layers & layers—
wrapping teeshirts around me as I stand in a public place—
more shirts, but bundled up & wrapped around my waist—
then more—I am growing larger—piling cotton jerseys on me,
dark colors—making a shelf like a plateau on me & hills & a
new Western landscape of me—I am larger & maybe 3 times me—
hills of shame and canyons.

I close an old brown raincoat around me & tie it to hold me in—
I feel a little safer—

       I had just remembered my mother's hairbrush
large & porcelain—metal & beautiful but scary—
everything in a set w/comb & mirror & well-ordered—
& now bodies around me as I walk into
the sea of people.

A woman making a noise of disgust with her mouth—*tstt*—
looks me up & down—*look at her*—*what is she doing*—to her male friend
& *you have a good body*—she says to me.

     ***

    I need this—I say—

     ***

I see all the metal bar beds in the orphanage & the dark & I need this
coat & this large body.

I pray for help from my father as I walk. I put on his VFW cap
—with its US Navy anchor pin.

Where is my father since he died? *Please come*—

I think of the word, "Resolute"/I think of the road, " Recompense."

& he comes, he shows as a large red cardinal around the corner
of a brick, 2-story house. His feathers a strong comb—Kingly.

Not like my mother's comb—with its stabbing teeth—the hitting brush—no,
he's red & alive & flying—

& he flies to a maple tree & starts to talk—*you will be okay*—*just keep going*—

Yet I'm afraid to walk among people—I don't feel safe—

The cardinal is saving me—singing its trilling song of salvation
to the trees.

My father's head emerges from the cardinal—
you are okay

& then he turns into a singing bowl

& with this redbird vision

I have become my own sacrament.
I start my songs with a low rasp.

No one will ever mistake me again—I am sturdy—large—
my new mountain body—not lumpy but filled with peaks to climb—

my body is land—
now I'm guttural, I'm loud in myself,

nothing ordinary or collapsing anymore—My mind is a slingshot—
just ammo, ready to fly.

I'm growling, gravelling into blues shouts:

> *Who will try me now?*
> *Who will come at me now?*

My Father Flying

The year after my father died,
I walked around to his places.
Not the cemetery, but to his people.
The Texaco where he took
his old Ford Fairlane for repair,
½ mile from the house.

I lugged two six packs of Iron City
to the mechanics—Chuck just out
of high school and older Joe, his round
belly hanging over his belt, so big
he rested it on the cars like a second body.
We told stories until the beer was gone.

I walked into my father's VFW,
Elmer J. Zeiler Post #5012, said
I was my father's daughter.
Good man, the old bartender said.
The two slumped-over vets at the bar
bobbed their heads and raised their beers.

After that, I saw my father flying.
In the trees by the old roads—a glimpse,
a wind shudder in the red maple
while everyday people kept walking
behind the shopping center.
A white patch in the December branches.

I'd pull over and look, and knew
he lived in the bends and curves,
the familiar sky, everywhere.
That was the year I looked up.
In that year after—
he was living everywhere.

Blood Ring

I cut a tunnel through my father's onyx ring,
cut the diamond out & stone-fired a garnet
in the center. My astrologer said that onyx
& diamonds together cool down love.
When I asked the jeweler not to clean
the band & bridge so my father's DNA
could bleed into my skin, he became stone,
looked at me like I was a baby-eater or pod person.
On my middle finger for a direct line to
the heart & years later I wandered into
Dynamic Energy Crystals in Sausalito, past
the singing bowls & the rose quartz globes.
The in-house psychic walked straight over
& said, *What is that ring?*
I told her it was my father's &
she said, *The energy goes through
that center stone & down into your body—
it's a channel.*
I looked down at the blood red opening.
It's a very powerful ring, she said,
I was very close to him, I said,
feeling the red spreading, feeling
the blood move, she felt it from
across the room:
I looked into her blue crystalline eyes,
I could see waves of air & other oceans.
Wear garnet on Saturdays, she said,

within one hour from sunrise during
the period of Saturn.
Okay, I said, rubbing the stone,
her standing so close I was feeling the ghosts
move through me in this crystal house
of meteorites & geodes,
this blood ring,
my father all around me.

Psych Intake w/ Flames

The tests say I have a high IQ but I have trouble
walking around—there are pins in the air
and so much pressure.

The nurse says, *Have there been any changes?*
I've been getting stoned a lot, I say.
I mean, your address, phone, insurance, she says.

I ask my shrink if something serious is wrong
with me. I think I'm a horrible person.
He says, *Your diagnosis is that you are super-human.*

I tell him I drink Pedialyte and like the texture of
baby food. I'm freaking out. I can't even talk
and eat at the same time.

For years I've been wearing men's clothes,
even though I don't like men:
Ely Cattlemen Gentlemen shirts, and ropers

from King's Saddlery in Wyoming—
I think, sometimes, you just have to say, okay—
even if you don't understand.

Sometimes, let the world of flames speak
for itself.

Let the radiant life shine.

What He Said

In line at the Swissvale Post Office,
he kept petting his long,
gray ponytail.

He turned and said:
I'm on my way to see my people.
Haven't seen them for a lot of years.

Wanna go with me?
I'm an Algonquin Indian, he strangely said—
my people are in Canada north of Quebec.

What? I said.
With his fringe suede jacket, he looked
like no one else in the post office.

I got two cases of Yukon Jack
for camping up North.
The others in line were starting to listen:

the woman in the brown wool coat gripping
rubber-banded envelopes, the guy with finger
tattoos and steel-toed boots.

Oh, yeah, that should be fun, I said.
His eyes were heavy brown.
So, you'll go, then?

No, no,
I'm not going, I said,
but I hope you have a great time.

Well, he said, *human beings are changing*
at the DNA level.
Is that right? I said.

Everyone loves a loaded gun, he said,
then stepped to the counter:
Two pages of Elvis stamps.

Then he left, casting the door open wide,
his fringe swinging in time with his long stride,
laying open the holster rawhided to his thigh.

In the shifting winter air between doors, he turned
and said: *If you come, you'll meet my ancestors,*
the dead will be there too.

Lowrider

Anthony was a lowrider, silver fire running
up his leg. We 3rd graders flamed as the nuns
came running in their black orthopedic shoes:
Where's Anthony?
All 20 of us lined up for the bathroom walk,
turned as we heard him scraping
down the tiled hall. Heard him dragging limp
in the silver brace that ran outside his pant leg,
around his heavy black shoe and up
to his knee. A shining steel,
his own metallic flame shooting
up his leg, the side panel of
the body, and in his high-gravel voice,
he said, *I'm here.*
You're late, said the nun jailers,
the fat of their arms hanging like weird fruit
or weapons, sheathed in the sleeves
of black habits: *Anthony, you have to keep up—*
you can't use your leg as an excuse—
and the flames went spiking and
punishment came as if by tribunal:
the low murmur spread through the line
of uniformed 9 yr olds:
They took his shoe!
They're making him walk in his sock.
Anthony, crying now,
his brace shining as the sun hit

through the '50s paned windows.
We all moved slowly toward him,
low and slow, a long snake.
Just look up! we said,
and everybody looked up,
our hearts flaming.
We were glimmering.
We were metallic.
We rolled on to the water fountain,
and they couldn't even see our engines,
450s with a dirty hum as we glided
past, leaving them
in their wrecked house of religion.
We saw sparrows through the paned windows,
free and flying in formation.
Anthony's brace scraping/
his sock-foot sliding,
and we let loose:
the biggest shot of renegade air,
hydraulics pumping, arriving together
while the nuns huddled in their cruelty
by the classroom door, holding
a crippled boy's shoe.

Leaving Iowa City

I needed a job, needed to get away
from the headcases of the over-educated,
I crossed town to the biker bar where
the backlot of Harleys, the beat leathers
and chain wallets made sense. I left
the professor in the famous writing workshop
wearing spaghetti-strap dresses,
who changed class time to suit her babysitter—
and when the student said she
couldn't make the time change, the professor
shrugged, her whole dress moving up/down with
red spaghetti snakes. I needed something to hold me
to the ground:

                    get beers for the bikers,
pick up trash in the backroom, watch the deadbeat
manager jerk-off to porno in his docksiders.
Better than the other professor who asked what
we read this summer, the students talking about
when they lived in Europe and how they just had to
read *The Cantos*—again. I'd rather spill pitchers on
the college frats in their plaid shorts, wear
the black apron to catch mayonnaise, sprays from
the soda gun. Pick up keys/glasses/condoms/
clean the urinal, everything steamy/
suffocating/teeming/afraid my poems
wouldn't survive the bounds of privilege.

In this flat land of blue eyes and blond hair,
I slept with the first dark-haired boy I found.

        I did what I knew how to do:
blow the busboy in his 501s after
a 12-hour shift, suck on free ice cream and pass out
on the bar. Go crazy disco after-hours
at the gay bar full of Aldo and farmboys and
go home alone to watch Home Shopping Network
and wait for serial killers. No keys to the farmhouse
where my bedroom's the first room in, living
with a gardener and fiction writer. My job was
sleep with the boss in his baggy pants
(no fucking way)
suck up to the mangy cooks if I want
my food, joke with the hostess in her sad
vintage dress or she'll cry again,
take poems to the legendary writers and after
two months pack up whatever fit in my
'72 Pontiac Ventura and drive away,
leave the rest on the lawn.

The Earthmovers

Hart Island serves as the City's public
final resting place of over one million individuals.
—New York City Dept. of Corrections

May 5, 2020, the island is alive
with earthmovers.

Not shovels, but John Deere lifts the dirt,
opening the ground for Covid victims.

Who runs the earthmover?
Who stacks the bodies in the mass graves?

What's in his mind as he
digs the deep and long holes?

Does he feel more alive today
as he looks at Long Island Sound,

is there a shorebird in the mudflats?
As he jumps from his machine

he sinks into the muddy ground.
Hart Island is alive with the dead today—

the Thursday gazebo visits canceled,
so no way to stare out at the graves.

Fear rises like a bulldozer blade—
and lingers like a thousand pins,

a metal heart on the skin.
Can we go back?

Can we replay this to save people?
One shovel of dirt.

What lives in the spaces of dying?
One blade moving,

one bird across the East River.

4

starling

My wings flat,
perfect cardboard painted white
with lines for feathers.
The blue sky robes hung
heavy and terrifying on me,
dragging as I walked.
I was the angel in the school play,
the awkward body masquerading
on stage. Ten years old,
I was always dressing up
to be one of them—
not the angels, but the children.
Peeling my name off my tiny body,
I left it. I couldn't stay with them.
There was no ancient belonging,
no way forward. In some other
sky, I made my own stars
and I filled the sky night.
The other small bodies
moved from here to there on stage.
I remembered
what I had read in the dark
green encyclopedia,
in the fat red dictionary,
where my love
is never starless.
And so I could fly away.
And so I could walk and talk
among them
as if I were there.

Spoonful

after Howlin' Wolf

Dear Mr. Wolf, your grinding, gravel voice
wrecks me down to disappearing & I know
Willie Dixon wrote "Spoonful" but you sell it w/
your whole body growl, massive hands on the
filigreed '50s mic in the Memphis clubs where
they made you use the back door, your body
bigger than the frame. Mr. Wolf, tree of a man,
how do you reach down inside? Pull up the howling &
you're dangerous, you're dangerous, wearing a skinny tie:
It could be a spoonful of diamond
It could be a spoonful of gold
You make me feel my body, I'm vibrating blue
I'm a ray of light, alive with the tenderness
that travels with burning—I want to be inside someone,
please help me be lost to myself &
emerge as another.
Willie said it wasn't about dope,
but when I heard "Spoonful," I went back—
the first time I did heroin with jesus freaks in
the bathroom stalls of the Stanley Theater—
Mylon LaFevre in his full-length fur & hot
as fire but clean & saved.
Mylon of Alvin Lee & Ten Years After, back
to the jesus concert in Pittsburgh where I sat in front &
he sat next to me, told me stories of hanging
with George Harrison & the Maharishi in India & how
he was saved—

Are you saved? he said.
Not yet, I said,
but all I could see was his perfect jaw,
his blue eyes drilling me, then his slide outside
to his '63 Lincoln w/suicide doors.
But Mr. Wolf, it's not rescue—
it's deliverance I want, the high in your lowdown
howl, '45 in your throat, flanked by Hubert Sumlin on
strat, Willie Dixon on upright bass, everyone
says there's nothing like heroin & that's true—
I wanted to float the disappearing dream & I got it—
then 3 days dopesick & no gravel to hold onto,
just the lack the wish the cold floor—
The bent strings of your semi-hollow Epiphone *that*
spoon that spoon, that . . . .
Fret against the mic stand dirty you stroking
a wooden spoon against the rising pleat
of your gabardine pants I love you
for that, you, inside
that growl, *that spoon,*
that spoon, that

. . . .

Green Comets of Future

Down County Road 18 outside of Stow,
my head flying the room of strangers.
I was fifteen & doing peyote in some guy's trailer,
buttons of weed, young enough I was

wearing my scapula around my neck,
burning into my skin with its green string, praising:
IMMACULATE HEART OF MARY,
PRAY FOR US NOW in all scary caps.

On the other side, Mary in long robes holding
this flaming bloody heart—
The green comets of future spinning,
catapulting me in & out of time &

I thought about my pillowcases at home, sewn
into a sleeping bag for safety, the drapes pinned shut.
Birds were flying around inside me—
in circles, white. Were they spirits returning

to dive-bomb the monstrous buildings of my past?
In the cloud soup, in the cloud river
of my brain, the hills & factories of Pittsburgh
rose up like the only real things.

What was it that people wanted from me?
What was I trying to hold together?
I hurtled the broken-down steps
of the single-wide—what passed for a

country home on that green night,
I could feel the psychopathic swirling of air,
my head now the comets, my head
now walking away.

Outlaw Dead

I want my dead to know I miss them/
well, some of them/

Is that a question the dead would entertain?

I want my dead to be alive to me,
as they walk the galactic stairs, threading the rungs
of the revenant storm & the rain's eye.

Oh mary mother of god,
there's a radio in their heads for communication
a frequency only shared by the outlaw machines.

There are missing pieces mary mother of god,
if they were any more wound up, they'd be

a timex, they are the mouth of the manhole

If You Slice the Moon

If you slice the moon in half
        shotgun pellets will spill into sky
        and rename beauty.

That's what I've seen.
        People running away from their inside fires.
        You can't blame them—

But they are losing life-color,
        becoming patterns of their former selves,
        into the blueness that's not really blue.

I'd rather be terrified.
        In the moving life
        that's running without me.

I can hear it.
        I'm breathing in it.
        Right now.

Now I call this my new beautiful
        because the terror is too large,
        too unseemly.

Can I flip the moon over and name it
        a piece of cloistered beauty?
        If I do, will it leave me?

My Father's Bandages

In the yellowed photo from the '40s,
my father wrapped in a hip-sling, a half-
dress, his 140 lb body gleamy with sweat,
almost dripping, his hands covered in bandages.
He's looking straight into the camera,
a cigarette to his mouth, a half fuck you/
half smile, the jungle of Papua New Guinea
behind him. You might not know it's
World War II, it's the Seabees, that my
Dad said it was the most beautiful place
he'd ever seen. "Jungle rot," he said,
"everybody had it. You just worked
with the bandages."
What was he thinking?
Now, when I look at him,
there's a river of light around him.
What breaks my heart may be
the same thing that breaks yours—
or not. Just know that he
was the builder, the one
before the Marines came,
and the scaffolding of bridges
and roads and buildings—
That can be a structure that slices
into night on the other side of the world,
a cutting away of light like an eclipse:
the branches of the body and the light:

is the light primary or the branch?
"If you ever get a chance,
go there," he said.
Oh Father, oh bandaged man
in the yellowed photo,
saving wire of light in this
partial night.

Sky Door

When I show my Dad the photos from the trip,
he lay on the couch covered by an afghan.

He turns the photos over to the white side:
Oh, he says in a weak voice, *these are nice.*

What does he see in the white?

Is he halfway to the other world & a sky door
pulling him through?

Dear Father: so much you were alone with—

I show you these photos but now
you take a hard right to your elemental song,
as your internal light of weeping fades.

I hope the whiteness is the hand of night
in charge of your new flight.

a man leaves his post & his body takes over

& then more bodies & more—

no sky   no job   no god   no authority—

just breath, the great ruler—

& a moment in a concrete warehouse
is everything—

the summer my father taught me fire.

& the bodies of the steelworkers
weld into one—

& the city of questions sleeps—
& the steel flakes in the lungs speak
& the outside law falls null & void—

when my father punches out his foreman at the mill:
awake in himself—

snaking

running downhill, bushes alongside
　　　　in your pf flyers, no shirt—
you're 12, beating all the boys, sting
　　　　of the pine tree as it scrapes
your arm. no language to hurt you, any
　　　　sting a gift next to the talk
of the stupid boys with their big hands.
　　　　you always win. you don't know
your body yet, but you use it. run.
　　　　follow the line of roadway to the next
blacktop. follow the curves to the snaking
　　　　river inside you. fly to the starless
night inside you. fast as you can with
　　　　scratched arms and bruises from
falling. you are a small god. inimitable.
　　　　beat them every time.

California

Around here, trees are hats,
little bowlers, van gogh lids of blown
divi trees that lean sideways
for the better view—
toppers, kangols, pork pies, wig hats.

I woke to the racket hailstorm:
little funnels of green at the edge of the hillside—jutting
out over the sea—the lives of people closeted
inside—who are they? Everyone's simple sorrow
writes a book a day—fills the hearts
of us with such pathos, bravery—&
then the small cruelties—
How do we speak to each other? I will never
meet the man in the shack on the hill.
Is he someone I should know?
Someone I could love?
Beauty assaults us until we say *no, no.*
It hurts to take in such brightness—
no, no—the cruelties, so familiar—are not
as bad—they are daily & interwoven.
How to know where to walk?
Space will give you the air you crave—even
the trees are reaching for a view—because
the splendor is devastating in its scope & depth—

———

I'm in the shadowlands of memory—
it's comforting in its grayness—there is
nothing stellar here—just the clank of the
ordinary machine, working—&
repeating—but its gears are marvelous in
their relationship & I know I can't really be
with another person—
we are all so covered in our own language
& dreams—no way thru—& great loneliness
is the human condition—but why?

————

I want to stay in the picture—
in the trees—comfort of having a ground, sense
of the growling biology & its laws—beyond me &
it rules me—takes the choices away—good.
No more this if this, that if that.
I need to sleep a while.

————

Sheets of rain—sideways—
gray rain sky—Pittsburgh in California—
but this is a wet gray—watercolor gray
with blue in it—
soft gray like an ocean
in the sky—beautiful.
Look again in the blue dream book.

The sadness of being so wrong about someone—
is it the sadness of no ground?
How am I so blind?

You will find me
with the tendons & arteries.

There is no law—but one must strive
to find the law—& then lie with its breaking—
each time—body/blood/moving/regeneration—
Dear house of great miracle
& pain & lethargy—
     I loved your laws—
your belief, your sweetness is incomparable—
I have to leave you for the open road & new beliefs—
detachment is not an option or desire in this life—

——in in in——

until you crack split wish you could go back back back—
to that time of bronze rich soil and great announcements—
the only sorrow is finding how solitary we are —how
unmoored

Around here, trees are hats, little bowlers, van gogh lids of blown
divi trees that lean sideways for the better view—

Sky Dog

Cancel my subscription to the resurrection.
—Jim Morrison

Doug sent me a golden gingko leaf in the mail—
in a dancing ninjas envelope & a *Lucky in Life,*
Reckless in Love card—a large woman in a straw hat &

blue rhinestone cat glasses in an old-school bathing suit.
Sealed with a stamp of a Japanese maidservant by
Eishōsai Chōki, designer of ukiyo-e woodblock prints.

I wander the house thinking of burning—
what marks us & what stays?
Soon the light will blaze the side window.

It's the thin, delicate gingko that survives,
even under siege in San Francisco fire & virus.
What is worth resurrecting?

A guy I know wears the face of his first love,
a 3×5 tattoo in blazing colors, covering his neck.
He walks the streets of the neighborhood &

tells his story of leaving her at the airport
in Saigon & how his body churned with being
torn from her. Sometimes I see him on the street

pointing at his neck, gesturing. The war, he
was young, & see her hair, liquid dark. Then
he shows his Sky Dog tattoo,

Duane Allman on his arm after his
bike wipeout in '71. His only two loves, he says.
Duane's long wild hair in faded blue,

with Sky Dog repeating in a circle around him.
Wilson Pickett gave him that name, he says,
and Hendrix died 3 years later.

Sometimes he slides a photo of his love
from the army jacket he still wears.
See her delicate flower dress.

Him 50 years younger in uniform,
his thick body beside hers, & now
she's on & inside him.

He built an altar to her in his front room,
with angel stones & a fire wheel to cleanse
the karma & honor those passing.

When he tells me the story the first time,
he's alive with her, sparks flying out
from his body as he speaks her name, after not seeing her

for five decades. His fire splatters me, sets me ablaze.
It's a love wildfire & I'm in it, my clothes
are gone, my eyes have changed. My body moves

differently, slides in the knowing story of his love.
In the new poem he wrote for her:

>*I dream your dress*
>*at the airport, last time*
>*as the fire wheel spins*

He slips the photo slowly in the combat
sleeve pocket, zips his jacket to cover her.
He walks her to the park for his daily resurrection.

Father, Blue Room

When he died,
his body was marked with sadness & blue, right after—

•

The unbearable flatness of the hospital curtains.

•

There was no real anything, just waves,
waves, & shades of cornflower.

•

Light all over the room,
the white bed.

•

Touching his forehead, his hand
no warmth.

•

Touching his forehead, his hand.

•

Arms of light across the bed
holding everyone I loved in the world.

•

The blue curtains & what used to be the sun:
a hundred fires burning in the window.

Dream Letters

The paper listed the ordinary things:
"Testing Site, Duquesne" and "School System, Carrick."

I opened the back of the diploma's frame and found
some notes inside in my father's handwriting.

The pins on his VFW cap that I touch as I enter my office
from the heart of dislocation, from the dead.

The elation and feeling of being
in his presence again was palpable:

the ordinary things:
testing site, school system.

My father received his GED
at the age of 61, nine years before he died.

Lung cancer from working in the mills,
it becomes clear my father is still here.

My father had to drop out of high school.
It was 1933.

In the tenth grade to get a job in order
to help support the family.

He enlisted. The Navy Seabees in WWII,
then laboring as a steelworker,

my father went back to school.

The paper said, "School System, Carrick,"
the paper said there was a dream that was real.

3 babies driving, zig-zaggy

'54 Pontiac traveling West along the sightlines
between the Sangre de Cristo Mountains
and the Joshua Tree Trail.

3 babies driving, zig-zaggy
on their way to their beginnings in dirt,
Black Eagle Mine Road,
dressed in all the clothes they wore
in their past life, dropping them
as they went: at Tucumcari
a white flowing shirt.

Someone's work apron left waving
on the metal hook in the Texaco,
Highway 104 West to Las Vegas, New Mexico.

At Rock Island, they crossed the train tracks dagger-like:

> over—over,
> over—back.

& the rattle of boards jarred them to this life,
the vibrations woke them
to their own blood & knowing.

3 babies—not yet crying—3 old souls
with many bodies between them,
in the full air of other floating bodies,
remembered tombstones of
the recently dead with the same name.

As my friend Heather said,
Martin Conroy,
halfway down the mountain of their birth.

As you might say,
the name of your dead,

further down the mountain,
toward the eagle, the jade area
and the green minerals.

The meridians of crossing this
longitude of dreams will carry you through,
holding you like a first mother.

When they arrived—
the Pontiac dissolving into space
and the bodies flying.

The in-between is left—
and the breaths
filled the moving river,
the air patterns.

Currents—and everything got thicker,
wilder, ready to burst from the inside
out—life and no way to trace it—
track it, account for it—
but only to know it in the blood—
in the old ways, the elemental crawl

of the burst, the settle,
then spark again—
you know it, but you can't reach it—
a slight breeze that feels like you felt it before,
a figure, white window in a dream that's
not really a dream—
your lives, your sightlines.

Turning wheel, take a drink before turning—

as you join the stream—it's the trauma
in you, in your walk, your bones,
your eyes—land of the pines—
see the headlights of your life—
southbound—

The sway of it—
thermals of the heart—
Heather & the rock:
the strip-racing-flags-of-air-
blow-it-off-your-back-
bright highway.

6

Those Night Roads, Wyoming

Those night roads that span long
in the dark through the foothills—

with only the tail lights of a far-off car
to lead you for light

That wild loneliness and hill freedom

and in the long distance another road
with blue light behind it

Is it the sky haze from a half-gone town
against the black dark?

Cutting the landscape in two—
those night roads

To the Woman at the Laramie Airport

Coming off a prop plane from Denver,
3rd flight of the day, I hit Laramie at 10:30
and it's pretty shutdown. Woozy, I'm fumbling
with luggage and the bolted metal gate at car rental,
a woman next to me in a heavy brown coat
the color of West. She's close,
head tilted and blue eyes tired like mine.
Do you need help? she says.
Yeah, I say, *it says to write down
my credit card number and slide it
under the gate. Where I come from,
that's a really bad idea.*
Oh, it's fine, she says, *that's how they
do it here—it's safe.*
Really? I say, but don't believe her.
I do it all the time, I live here, she says,
where are you going?
Coming on to midnight, I look hard
at this stranger, tell her I'm on my way
to a residency up at Brush Creek.
Oh, how wonderful, she says, seems
like she means it, her voice high with excitement.
She was happy for me.
She told me the way to the rental lot,
I thanked her and washed my face.
Still, I got lost in the dark, and when I
reached Lot G7, she was standing in

my spot. I'm thinking stalker, *Single
White Female*. She's going to rip my throat
with my own keys, stuff my body in the trunk.
*I told you the wrong place
for the car*, she said.
Oh thanks, I said.
She helped me with my bags,
Have a great residency, she said—
thanks, really—thanks, I said.
So tired I couldn't figure out the car—
they told me to get 4-wheel drive for
the back roads and the snow.
So when I took the airport exit,
she pulled out ahead about 20 yards,
blinked her headlights, her arm out
the driver's window a 90-degree pivot
and turned right onto Snowy Ridge Road
towards Laramie—I turned left.
I beeped and waved.
She didn't have to do it.
Two women at night in the night
of the world. She saw me with no bearings,
she saw me afraid, she stepped up and
loved a stranger. She didn't have to
do any of it.

Half-Sun over Powder River

for Don

Half-sun over the Big Horns—white clouds graze the foothills
and you're on my mind. Your skin on mine,

voice sleepy low: *I'm resting my eyes* as you fall deep into me.
Light beneath the clouds an alien breakthrough,

string dream to the sky. If you fly that shimmering
to Powder River, running down from the high plains,

you'll find that full-sun sky where sand looks like dust,
a dust that runs to the underground earth

where the three forks meet—the swirling below,
the fire circle, this sweet life with you.

Thunder Bay

The cormorant at the ferry dock.
No people, but I was surrounded by the living.
5AM, Prince Rupert, British Columbia,
needed to wait till 6
for the ferry office to open, and the water
and fog and bird left me with
the cab driver's words:
It depends on the water,
when I asked about the ferry schedule,
and when I told him about my Canadian father
he whirled around in his seat, his eyes burning
into me, his arm reaching at me:

> *You have to look for him*
> *You have to do this*

I sat on the bench where Yellowhead Highway ran
to the sea, my body burning
its own rageful light—and there was no time, no sight,
there just was—in that pure moment of being where we
show our hearts —the stillwaters outside press
the only law of one body against another.

> How would I find him?
> —no rest until I knew him and
> where he stood—
> A moment with this stranger on Highway 16
> and now awake in myself—

I rode the ferry to the train across Canada,
running through Terrace and Edmonton, through Winnipeg,
not knowing it was my father's birthplace—
and on to Saskatoon, Sudbury—
And finally Thunder Bay, along the top of
Lake Superior, where the land breaks
into ancient outcroppings, running into the Sleeping Giant
and the bedrock of the Canadian Shield—

and that's when Lily came on board,
her blue ribbon with white lace, clipped
to long brown hair—her almost vertical smile
rising into her thin face, and the mystical true
came alive, she was my stranger, sister—
and we talked, laughed silly
from Thunder Bay to Toronto. I stayed
in her apartment, wildly stoned, waiting for
my train home the next day. Not wanting
to pull away from her, I could feel the bones
of her thin shoulders, I could feel the call
of Union Station just blocks away, her soft hands
brushing my face as in leaving, she took her light
blue ribbon and clipped it in my hair.

       I thought I would see her again—
       I thought I would find my way back—

I hold her ribbon, some thirty years gone,
in my writing desk, rising from that ferry dock
and the cormorant, the burning fog of
my father, the law of her body against
mine, in Thunder Bay.

Scarline

On any given day, they would lock me up.
I miss those hills of the body,
the line bruises from slamming the edge
of the dresser—

Those lines of demarcation are the scarlines
of hurricanes:
new continents rising to the surface:
this happened here
this girl lived

——

I was a split baby/
      half a body here, half
      nowhere

—asylum baby

split off
with the dull
tools
of the cutters.

——

I stayed
until birds flew out of me
until words became animals

———

Mothers
selling us to
strangers with a wallet—

and the walking bodies say:
when I saw you, I knew
you were mine.

I'm not yours.
You can't own a split thing.

———

I found the cheap gold cross you sent,
buried under papers and books.

The letter where your priest told you:
Adoption is God's work.
I don't know if you're still alive.

Bloodmother, finding you was like finding religion,
but without the cruelty and deception—
but then, what's left?

———

Only:
Continents   landforms   upsurges

In this split kingdom
this body walk of life,
I'm the scarline.

Road to Ketchikan, 1987

Spent my last money
to see the Turner exhibit in San Francisco,
so I could watch the lone figure walk into light.
I wanted that—not death—
but that walking into/not knowing
who will emerge.

A week later, I found myself in the hull,
in the big ship
on the Alaska Marine Highway,
in a circle with the first mate, some
shipmen, & the captain stretched
out his big hand with a bottle of Yukon Jack.

We were rolling on to Ketchikan,
hanging on through the open waters
of Prince William Sound—
when the great ship rolled & twisted &
plates of dinners slid off tables,
passengers clear-fell from chairs &

walkers grabbed railings to stay upright,
crawling to the sidewalls. Only six days ago,
Turner had opened me to time & light
but leaving land I felt the light rolling—
my body's inside body
spinning—my head dizzy &

I prayed for it to stop—
the open waters threw us like a mangled body,
like a child's boat, battered:
to be changed &
to live inside
the ocean dark.

A young shipman ran over, said,
Find a place & hang on.
He ran from body to body
helping with cuts & terrors.
No power but to wait,
I locked eyes with a boy of about eight

in a blue jacket, shivering.
An older couple lay on the deck,
clinging to the siderail.
After forty minutes it was over—
the boy ran crying, the couple kissed,
touching each other's faces, newly alive.

As aides checked the passengers,
the man helping me said, *C'mon, have a drink*,
& we climbed down the metal stairs
to the bowels of the ship, to the room of gruff men.
Their uniforms dirty & pulled away from the day's
turbulence, their voices thick with the still fear

& victory of it: they passed the whiskey.
One man whose eyes gleamed blue
in the dark room said,
Are you traveling alone?
Yeah, I'm a poet.
I'm going to a writer's conference in Sitka.

Do you know Robert Service? he said.
I have his book with me, I said.
They cheered & raised the bottle & in the black dark
of the crowded hull, they started to recite:
There are strange things done in the midnight sun
By the men who moil for gold;

That night as we steered to the Inside Passage,
the ghosts pulled the words from their own deep,
from the low place of the buried dead:
The Arctic trails have their secret tales
That would make your blood run cold;
How did I get to this sea, this hull of time?

Louder, & they knew the words
like they lived them—
raising their muscled arms
that lifted the cargo of years:
. . . that night on the marge of Lake Lebarge
I cremated Sam McGee.

7

Drag Strips

Four lines of a lyric

(or nothing comes that rises):

Dear figure of mother: I'm staying

with the white page: since

nothing comes that rises—

just the truth that drags & bitters

When I Was Holy

The first time I was holy my birthmother
gave me a cheap plastic bottle of water
from Lourdes with a red cap.

Holy not because of the water, not because
she said, *Oh, I'll get that for my little bastard baby,*
—but the handing over,

that perfect cinematic moment
that birthed the expanding, the breathing
water in me.

I'm across the street from the sea,
years later at the Miami oceanwalk and the green
art deco they used in *Scarface*,

right where Tony Montana shot the Colombian
on the steps, him clutching his orange bebop
shirt in his ratty drug-dealer shoes and the dramatic

stumble down the steps after the classic scene
with Marta and the sawed-off shotgun on the bed:
¡Quietó! ¡No te muevas, cabróncito!

Before the chainsaw and the bloody bulls-eye,
holy in its choreography but really its justice.
What is it you hand over?

The holy baby, the yayo, the fake miracle water?
When Montana assumes a shooting stance,
unloads 2 into the Colombian in the middle

of Ocean Drive, jumps in the car with sexy
Stephen Bauer, yelling *Go! Go!* is that holy?
On the oceanwalk, a Cuban band plays Bon Jovi,

"It's My Life," golf carts of tourists rolling by,
and the best stripshot of breeze I've ever felt.
I can't get to the start of it, the getting

born of it—but the middle much sweeter,
like cardamom, like rhubarb pastry,
which I don't like, but the berry color

feels free. You tell me what holy is.
I say the waiter with a smooth low:
Hey beautiful, don't lift the tray.

I don't want you to work.
Holy.
His white teeshirt, jeans, flat black shoes.

Miami palms in their sensual glide
to the sky. Holy.
Earth, sky,

breathing water. 1 bowl of love.
1 thing,
holy.

Now I'm a heart without a head, walking.
I don't need to be right—
I just need it to be worth it,

and I've got a finishing streak—
Everyone has their little gun,
but it's the sleeveshot of quiet I want.

I'll pull your arms over me,
I'll be wrong and wrong and wrong
as long as I can, loving you.

The Made: Train

Pink and white wildflowers Mile Marker 40
monster spools of industrial wire.
Lilypad/boulder/
I saw armies of bloodfathers,
you were breastplates and long-swords
and nothing could stop you—
not even the forest, the rocks—
I was the flailing one needing a way through—
The lilypads gleamed neon
in this otherworld dream.
Your eyes the fire on the hillside
shining my life
back to me.
You made me/
but I made you out of
clues from my body.
In the river—a long line of
8 ft grasses—wheat-colored—
a 50 yd line of it/
standing guard along the shore—
then the riveted rust-colored bridge//
rising up from the natural world/
the made.

Leaving Santa Fe

I've known disappearance, but never
4 AM corner dark with months of clothes
on my back. Past Nino's near St. Michael's
and Smith's grocery where I went daily
to trash talk with the bag packers about
hair and magazine covers, maybe
all those years of waitressing.

I've fucked men for years to disappear,
drugs for years to go missing,
hungry to be institutionalized
to have my choices removed—
looking for a pathway to sky
without dying, a way to not be here.
5:10 AM driving on Cerillos, the GPS

says *Sá-ril-oss* in the black dark.
No traffic but homeless people
on the sidewalk. One man pushing
a shopping cart piled high with stuff,
hard to make out in the shadows.
He's wearing a long raincoat, gloves,
even though it's 73 degrees.

Another guy on the corner just standing,
staring. I pull up beside him at the light,
his clothes hanging, pants dragging,
no movement. Some kind of Mexican
rap comes on the radio, one click and
my door locks. The DJ says it's
Roaring Lion doing "Spanish Calypso."

The knife pulled on me in the back room,
fucking him to avoid calling it rape,
living in my car— but not for long.
I've known disappearance,
moving 14 times in a year,
but what was the man on the corner
staring at?

I came to—in rooms I didn't recognize
with people I didn't know.
Never 4 AM corner dark
with months of clothes on my back.
I drove away from Cerillos
in my rental car, wishing him mercy,
my privilege running over me like water.

Dream Highway: Quarantine

In all the cities of this year
I have longed for the other city.
—Muriel Rukeyser

Dear striations of night:

show me the sky door

to my cities of leaving—

some track to the hammer forward

of my wrecked, ambitious

highway-of-dreams head.

The Jailer

Guy in the restaurant shouting:
No, I was never a baby, never!
I'm watching him waving
his hands, his chin-long black hair &
mustache moving as he calls at the air:

I told you I was never a baby!
In the way of pink blankets
swaddled with some mother,
I wasn't a baby either.
His 50-ish body wavering, small hands

in full tantrum hitting the restaurant air
like a gone lover.
A cook runs full-apron from the kitchen,
the owner from the front of the house—
they put their hands on him:

Stop this! Sit down!
      Who are you? he says,
      what are you doing?
I'm part of the frenzy now,
but keep it locked down like a jailer.

Who hurt him, what ripped him open?
Two security guards come
to take the man away.

I say nothing,
though I know the snap/

the spring open like a hinge/
hello hurricane,
hello man shouting,
I'll be the air:
never a baby, never.

•

It doesn't matter about the brain.
Jailer of the body, I live in the place where people that were never born live—
When the guards shunt the man past me, I see his one wild eye,
keeper of everything that couldn't be set right.

Miraculous

As a child I spent a lot of time in the closet. I sat, bent like a finger in arthritis.

Here I could become anything: a cloud, a C note, Michael Jackson's rhinestone hand.

By the time my mother would finally unlock the door to say, "Had enough?"

I was able to imagine her as someone miraculous, someone saving me

from my mother.

the river of light is all we have

she is an idea of a mother
she is the quiet part of weeping

she is skimming away

the reason you take a train West/
the reason you shift hard into 5th and take the turn rough

I decide to believe in her sky
because happiness fleeting is still happiness

the new ways not yet here,
not visible or known.

Notes

"The Emptying" refers to Rosalia Asylum and Maternity Hospital, an orphanage in the Hill District of Pittsburgh.

"Sanctified" is dedicated to Sister Rosetta Tharpe, who was known as the "Godmother of Rock and Roll." Her amazing fire and command of the stage influenced Chuck Berry, Elvis, and other early rock musicians. She crossed over from gospel to rhythm and blues, and her 1964 tour with Muddy Waters, especially her concert in Manchester, England, on May 7th is said to have influenced British blues players such as Eric Clapton, Keith Richards, and Jeff Beck.

The term "Blues Shouter" refers to singers who "belted out their songs at constant full volume . . . projecting a fervour and energy into their delivery." Some early Blues Shouters were Sister Rosetta Tharpe, Screamin Jay Hawkins, Howlin' Wolf, and many more. https://www.allaboutbluesmusic.com/blues-shouters/

"Blues Shouter" also refers to the voices of unknown bodies of women, the women who can no longer speak, the women whose voices are marginalized, the women who struggle to speak on a daily basis.

"Psych Intake w/ Flames" is for Nancy Kirkwood. It refers to Kings Saddlery in Sheridan, Wyoming, where you can buy Ely Cattlemen Gentlemen shirts, ropers, saddles, or just walk in and smell the best leather smell of your life.

"Spoonful" after Howlin' Wolf refers to the song by the same name. Sam Phillips said that Chester Burnett, the "Howlin' Wolf," was his favorite artist of all the blues artists he worked with at Sun Records. "Spoonful" was written by Willie Dixon, who helped to define the arc of Chicago electric blues. Some of Dixon's greatest songs were recorded by major artists at Chess Records in the '50s and '60s, such as "Hoochie Coochie Man" (Muddy Waters), "You Can't Judge a Book By the Cover" (Bo Diddley), "My Babe" (Little Walter), "Wang Dang Doodle" (Koko Taylor), "I Just Want to Make Love to You" (Etta James), and many more. In his autobiography, *I Am the Blues*, Dixon wrote, "People who think 'Spoonful' was about heroin are mostly people with heroin ideas." Instead, it was about sex, as Howlin' Wolf suggested on stage, enacting masturbation with a wooden spoon to his groin while singing. https://www.udiscovermusic.com/stories/howlin-wolf-spoonful/'Spoonful': The Story Behind Howlin' Wolf's Classic Blues Song

Mylon LeFevre began a life of music as a gospel singer born in Georgia. Elvis recorded one of his songs, "Without Him." LeFevre was part of Alvin Lee's great band, Ten Years After. They collaborated on the album *On the Road to Freedom* (1973) with guest musicians George Harrison, Steve Winwood, Jim Capaldi, Ron Wood, and Mick Fleetwood. He later started Mylon LeFevre Ministries. He was inducted into the Gospel Music Association Hall of Fame and the Georgia Music Hall of Fame.

"Skydog" is for Doug Powell. It refers to the nickname of slide guitar hero Duane Allman. His original nickname was "Dog," given to him by Rick Hall, founder of FAME studios in Muscle Shoals, supposedly "because he looked like an old hound dog with his big ears and hanging-down white hair." That nickname later shifted to "Skyman" when Allman was playing with Wilson Pickett in the Muscle Shoals sessions. As Hall said, "he loved to have a toke. He'd go in the bathroom, then come back and play his ass off." Eventually, "Skyman" and "Dog" kind of merged into "Skydog." https://lareviewofbooks.org/article/duane-allman-skydog-explained/Lary Wallace

"3 babies, driving zig-zaggy" is for Judith Vollmer.

"To the Woman at the Laramie Airport" is for Sharon Hawkins.

"Half-Sun Over Powder River" and "When I Was Holy" are for Don Hollowood.

"Scarline" makes use of language from the work of Diane Glancy, with thanks.

"The Jailer," with thanks to Ken Hart.

Acknowledgments

The author wishes to thank the following journals in which these poems first appeared, sometimes in earlier versions:

Academy of American Poets Poem-a-Day ("Drag"); *Agni* ("Lowrider"); *Allium* ("Dream Letters"); *The Atlantic* ("The Body's River"); *Barrow Street* ("What He Said"); *Catamaran* ("Blues Shouter"); *Cherry Tree* ("The Jailer," "When I Was Holy"); *Copper Nickel* ("Dragstripping"); *Florida Review* ("The Stripping Tools"); *Great River Review* ("If You Slice the Moon," "I Ran Into Water," "Junkie," "Leaving Santa Fe," "Miraculous," "Scarline"); *Kestrel* ("a man leaves his post & his body takes over," "the river of light is all we have"); *Lip* ("Outlaw Dead"); *Narrative Northeast* ("Drag Strips," "Green Comets of Future," "The Emptying"); *Ocean State Review* ("Spoonful"); *Paterson Literary Review* ("Blood Ring," "Father, Blue Room," "My Father Flying," "Road to Ketchikan, 1987," "The Made: Train"); *Pedestal* ("California"); *Quartet* ("To the Woman at the Laramie Airport"); *San Diego Poetry Annual* ("Dream Highway: Quarantine," "Leaving Iowa City," "Snaking," "The Earthmovers," "Those Night Roads, Wyoming"); *Shenandoah* ("Skydog," "The Drawbridge"); *South Dakota Review* ("My Father's Bandages," "Psych Intake w/Flames," "Starling," "When Rape Was An Ocean"); *Southern Indiana Review* ("Sanctified"); *Tahoma Literary Review* ("Thunder Bay"); *Valparaiso Poetry Review* ("Half-Sun over Powder River").

A number of these poems appeared in the chapbook *Skydog*, published in 2022 by Lefty Blondie Press.

I would like to express my appreciation to the Pennsylvania Council on the Arts; the Pittsburgh Cultural Trust and the Howard Heinz Endowment and Laurel Foundation; the Pittsburgh Foundation; the Creative Capital Foundation; the Dodge Foundation; the Betsy Hotel Residency and Florida International University; the Brush Creek Ranch Residency; the Folger Shakespeare Library, Lit Youngstown, the MacDowell Colony; Joyce Jenkins, Richard Silberg and Poetry Flash; Allison Adelle Hedge Coke and the Platte River Whooping Crane Trust; The Poetry Center Passaic County Community College; Santa Fe Arts Institute; Storyknife Writers Retreat; Ucross; and Leighton Studios, Banff, Alberta; the Warhol Foundation for fellowship and support that helped me to write these poems. Thanks to excellent editors Terrance Hayes, Nancy Krygowski, Jeffrey McDaniel and the wonderful staff at the University of Pittsburgh Press who made this book possible, especially the fabulous Alex Wolfe, John Fagan, and Lesley Rains. Special thanks to Carlos Hernandez for his kick-ass artwork.

Thanks to the dragstrippers and blues shouters, and all the people who have helped me in so many ways with these poems, including Lisa Alexander, Maggie Anderson, Rick Barot, Ellen Bass, Joe Bathanti, Joan E. Bauer, Sandra Beasley, Robin Becker, Beeb, Kelley Beeson, Patty Bernarding, Betsy, Mike, and Quincy, the amazing Richard Blanco, Linda Blaskey, Bounce (extraplanetary brother of Don), Elizabeth Bradfield, Doralee Brooks, Mad Dog Brooks, Wild Jenny Browne, Sarah Browning, Daniella Buccilli, C. M. Burroughs, Elena Karina Byrne, Nicole Hefner Callihan, Gabrielle Calvocoressi, Peter Campion, Sheila Carter-Jones, Cortney Lamar Charleston, Jane Ciabattari, the most cosmic & wild Sandra Cisneros, Henri Cole, Kristofer Collins, Kay Comini, Jessica Cuello, the coolest Frank Czuri, Teri Cross Davis, Todd Davis, Tony Diaz, Tamara DiPalma (Tam-o), Kendra DeColo, Jennifer Kwon Dobbs, Heather Donohue, Sharon Doubiago, Damian Dressick, Mary Alice Drusbasky, Denise Duhamel, Iris Jamahl Dunkle, Lynn Emanuel, Martín Espada, Martin Farawell, Dr. G., Angela Gaito-Lagnese, RJ Gibson, Maria Mazziotti Gillan, Aracelis Girmay, Diane Glancy, Donna Greco, Tim Green, David Groff, George Guida, Dr. H., Linda Aluise Haberman, James Allen Hall, Bill Harding, Ken Hart, Sharon Hawkins, Allison Adelle Hedge Coke, Amy Lee Heinlen, Ruth Hendricks, Niki Herd, Faith Hill, Brenda Hillman, Jean Hadfield Hollowood, Bob Hoover, Jenny Johnson, Michael Jones, Dr. K., Colleen Keegan, the fabulous Nancy Kirkwood, Peter Kline, Nancy Koerbel, Yusef Komunyakaa, Nancy Krzton, Beth Kukucka for inspired photography, Carl Kurlander, Gerry LaFemina, Gail Langstroth (mudfire), Dorianne Laux, ML Liebler, Gary Copeland Lilley, Diane Lockward, Michael Lotenero, the Madwomen, Marilyn Marsh Noll, Adrian Matejka, David Mayhew, Claire McCabe, Jane McCafferty, Patty McCollum, Lynne McEniry, Campbell McGrath, Bob McGrogan, Leslie Mcilroy, Rachel McKibbens, Marguerite Miller, Wayne Miller, Ron Mohring, Nikki Moustaki, Mihaela Moscaliuc, Diane Mrozowski, Peter Murphy, Liane Ellison Norman, Deena November, Jean O'Brien, Bill O'Driscoll, Alicia Ostriker, Wendy Paff, Dorina Pena, Bonita Lee Penn, Brittany Perham, Lee Peterson, Beth Piraino, Michelle Politiski, Cherise Pollard, D.A. Powell, Peg Alford Pursell, Deb Pursifull, Ruben Quesada, Nancy Bank Raffetto, Anne Rashid, John Repp, Suzanne Roberts, Dr. Robin, Lee Ann Roripaugh, Patrick Rosal, Gerry Rosella Boccella, Don

Rosenzweig, Todd Sanders, Nicole Santalucia, Susan Sailer, Sapphire, Karen Schubert, Naomi Shihab Nye, Joanne Samraney, Janet Sarbaugh, Fred Shaw, Matthew Siegel, Brian Siewiorek, M.A. Sinnhuber, Emily Mohn-Slate, Tom Sleigh, Patricia Smith, Tracy K. Smith, Shirley Snodey, Rhoda Mills Sommer, Dana Stabenow, Ann Tomer, Erin Hollowell, Maura Brenin and the wild women of Storyknife; Michelle Stoner, Michael Thomas, Tony Trigilio, Bernadette Ulsamer, Beatrice Vasser, John Vercher, Julie Marie Wade, Ellen Wadey, Stacey Waite, Michael Waters, Holly Watson, Afaa Michael Weaver, Anna Claire Weber, Patricia Jabbeh Wesley, Lesley Wheeler, White Whale Books, Marcus Wicker, Rachel Wiley, Sarah Williams-Devereux, Lori Wilson, David Wojahn, Laurin Wolf, poetry hero Michael Wurster, C. Dale Young, Zoe from Santa Fe, and many more. Remembering those who passed ahead: blues shouter Gary Belloma, Anita Byerly, Jimmy Cvetic, Patricia Dobler, Gayle Reed Carroll, Dorothy Holley, the irreplaceable Britt Horner, Jeff Oaks, Bob Patak, Jerry Stern, Lucienne Wald, Jill West; always R.T. Beatty, Big Jim Hollowood and the 40 ft. guitar, Vera Hollowood, Charlotte Thoma. A special thanks to the wild poet traveler, Judith Vollmer, the beloved Ed Ochester, and my true north, Don Hollowood.